Tough Skin,

Soft Heart

A Leadership Book About Growing Stronger, Better and Wiser

Shannon M. Cohen

Tough Skin,
Soft Heart

Published 2018
Printed in the United States of America

ISBN 978-1-939294-58-6

Published by splatteredinkpress.com

To every difference maker that continues to wake up, show up, and give the best of themselves in service to others
...this book is for you!

Thank you!

Acknowledgments

To my husband – You are one <u>AMAZING</u> man! You have always supported every dream and vision of my heart. I am so thankful that you daily invest all of you into loving all of me.

To my son – Even as a young man, I am astounded by your heart and sensitivity for the needs of others. You inspire many pages of this book. I hope testaments from my journey help you to cultivate tough skin while maintaining your tender heart. Humanity needs more of that.

To my family and friends – Thank you for walking alongside me in my own Tough Skin, Soft Heart journey and for allowing me to walk alongside you in yours. Your presence blesses my life!

To every #ToughSkinSoftHeart subscriber, client, and supporter – What began as a blog in 2014 has now blossomed into a book, and it's all because of you! Thank you for every email, social media comment, and word of thanks sharing tangible ways Tough Skin, Soft Heart has helped you navigate difficult moments in your life and leadership. I write inspired by you and in service of you.

Tricia L. McDonald, Julie Lankes and the BoxBoom Creative Team, Anna J. Roseboro, Michele Stitt, and Melinda Clynes – An author's ultimate dream team! Thank you for sharing your gifts with me in my journey to publishing my first manuscript. You ladies ROCK!

Introduction

Tough Skin,
Soft Heart

A leadership book about growing stronger, better and wiser.

Accept this introduction as a hug and personal letter of thanks from me to you. On behalf of all of the people, movements, communities, and organizations that you relentlessly give your life and support to...THANK YOU! The ripple effect of your life and leadership are felt even beyond the people who know you personally.

You're exactly the type of leader I had in mind when writing this book!

Tough Skin, Soft Heart is not your run-of-the-mill '85 Steps to Becoming a

More Phenomenal You' book. As far as I am concerned, you are already phenomenal. This book is about creating a space of respite, reflection, and renewal for already phenomenal folks who do pretty amazing things in service of others.

If you love, lead, or serve anyone at all, you've probably realized some of the same difficult truths I have: Life hurts. People injure. Disappointments arise. Mistakes get made.

This book is a guide for developing the resilience needed to successfully navigate the valleys of life and leadership. Each story and affirmation is designed to inspire you to awaken each day with renewed commitment to operate with integrity, pursue purpose, and exhibit compassion. Leading from a place of excellence demands tenacity and resolve. You will be tested. Challenges will emerge and show what you are made of. Pressures will arise daily that push and pull against your very core.

We are all walking history books replete with narratives of setback and triumph, grief and relief, sorrow and surcease. Developing tough skin and cultivating a soft heart means not allowing what irks or hurts us to make us irksome, irritable, and bitter.

<u>Tough Skin, Soft Heart is about:</u>

- Merging intention and impact
- Bringing healing to the walking wounded
- Committing to self-love and ongoing personal growth
- Giving grace before you need grace
- Supporting leaders teetering on the brink of burnout

- Offering strength for the person whose feelings have seemingly been hurt one too many times

This book is about resisting the temptation to build walls that prohibit us from seeing the best in ourselves and the best in others when life or those in our lives hurt us. Tough Skin, Soft Heart living means refusing to give in to the temptation to lump and bundle all people into the 'no good' pile just because of encounters with a few 'ugly-acting' folks.

While I can't tell your story, I can share glimpses from my own journey. Tough Skin, Soft Heart is my open letter of love penned to encourage the hearts of difference makers like you. Within these pages, I share how I stay motivated to respond versus react, to refuse retreat when life gets hard, and to live each day with tougher skin and a softer heart. I hope that pages from my own leadership journal and journey serve as a springboard for your story. Read and be inspired to reflect on what you need and what will help you in this season of your life and leadership.

On Reading Tough Skin, Soft Heart

Every leader needs daily space to retreat, rethink, replenish, and reflect. There are 31 entries in this book. You can read them all at once, or you can read one per day over the course of a month. Think of this book as a mini-retreat or getaway in the palm of your hand. Use it as part of your routine to help start your day from a space of mindfulness. Read it as a leadership warm-up exercise to impact the way you approach your work and those you lead. Use this book for a midday pick-up when the pressures of life and leadership mount. Or use it in the solace of your quiet time at the end of the day.

Let Tough Skin, Soft Heart be a springboard to initiate your own self-care and to inspire you to journal your own life lessons. While the book creates a safe place to be honest about the emotional toll and invisible price tag of leadership, this book is not exhaustive. The topics I do not mention create the perfect opportunity for chronicling your own story. Each entry ends with Tough Skin, Soft Heart action and reflection thoughts. These thoughts are affirmations, prayers, and to-do's all rolled into one. As you read - carve out the intimate space you need to listen to your heart, honor and check your emotions, validate your being, refresh your sense of purpose, and renew your commitment to lead.

Ultimately, this book is an anthem of the boldness and courage it takes to love, lead, and serve each and every day.

Thinking of you and thanking you for all you are and do!

Xoxo

Shannon

Table of Contents

Day 1
Frenemies

In 2009, President Obama entered the White House for his first day on the job carrying Doris Kearns Goodwin's *A Team of Rivals*, a biography about the leadership of Abraham Lincoln. A media buzz swiftly ensued as political pundits speculated about the symbolism of the President entering the Oval Office with that particular book in hand. The buzz reached such a high that media correspondents decided to interview the biographer herself.

During her interview, Goodwin discussed the two aspects of Lincoln's administration and leadership he was most famous for: The Emancipation Proclamation and his savvy in "frenemy" engagement. Lincoln positioned his biggest critics as cabinet members and his opponents were often members of his inner sanctum leadership circles.

I believe President Obama took Lincoln's biography into his first day on the job to signify his plan to strategically engage the frenemies he would inherit by default. Like Lincoln and Obama, every leader experiences 'frenemy' encounters and has to develop and implement a frenemy engagement strategy.

What is a frenemy?

I define a *frenemy* as an individual who respects and loathes you at the same time. Frenemies are as pervasive as air - they are everywhere, at times invisible, but their presence is always felt. A frenemy is someone with whom you may find yourself implicitly or explicitly in both competition and collaboration with. With frenemies, you can't tell when a compliment is actually a complaint. Frenemies are people who don't know if they really wish you well or just wish they thought of the idea first. Truth is, frenemies come in differing degrees and are more than polished versions of the proverbial "hater."

Frenemies:

- Are often our biggest critics and watch our every move

- Mysteriously find ways to travel in the same circles you do

- See qualities in us they like, admire, or respect, but for some reason, feel threatened by our light

- Stalk our social media sites, but never "like" a single post

- Want to stay close enough to witness, experience, and draw from our shine, but simultaneously resent, criticize, or devalue the light that radiates from us

- Can be family members, childhood friends, colleagues, board members, former coaches and mentors, and even people we only know by association

The best way to head off frenemy activity is by being proactive. Who are the frenemies in your circles? How can you strategically position yourself (and them) in a way that protects your heart, vision, and interests? Frenemies will be thorny no matter where they are, but being proactive may provide greater control in setting boundaries to control the level and extent of access frenemies have to you.

ONE LAST THING...

The human condition means that each of us has frenemy capacity. If we are not careful and in sync with checking our own behavior, emotions, responses, and motives, we can easily slip into frenemy mode with people we see walking in their purpose in ways we wish we were.

Tough Skin, Soft Heart Truth

Tough Skin: I will inventory my circles, social media, and spheres of influence to identify frenemy presence and activity. I may not be able to avoid or nullify the presence of a frenemy, but I will focus on ways I can protect myself and strategically neutralize frenemy activity in my life and leadership.

Soft Heart: Am I showing up in someone else's life as a frenemy? I will check my own behavior, emotions, responses, and motives towards others. I will not be jealous of someone else's success, gains, or wins. I will not be a source of nice-nasty behavior in the life of someone else. I will exhibit the same authenticity I want to receive. I will not be petty, spiteful, or speak ill of others. I won't grow mute at the sight of someone else's success.

Day 2
Behind the Veil:
The Secret Life of
the Frantic Leader

Dear Fellow Difference Maker,

I see you. I know you. I've been you... no,
correction: I AM YOU.

I know what it is like awakening to the
sound of the alarm clock, and with it the
triggering of a mental auto-pilot download
of a massive to-do list. I've felt the pressure
of a Google task list that screams
demanding attention before a shower has
been had or a pot of coffee made. I know
what it is like to feel as if pausing to sit and
eat during the day would be an
inconvenience and time stealer. There are

days, weeks, and whole seasons of life where it feels like there is never enough of me to go around. I know how it feels to constantly struggle with a deficit between hours in the day, what needs to be accomplished, and what I can give. I know that getting 'caught up' is code for an elusive pie-in-the-sky dream where email inboxes are cleared and messages responded to [not just tucked in folders]. I know that sometimes papers get stuffed in random drawers just to give the external appearance that all is as it should be. Somehow these well-manicured junk drawers become mini microcosms of our interior lives. We stuff things so all looks well even when life isn't well.

I've given myself the same pep talk. 'As soon as THIS project is over, I will_____ [fill-in-the-blanks]. I tell myself I will slow down, get balanced, find order, and reclaim my peace, just as soon as THIS project is successfully wrapped up. Yet somehow, life continues to morph into one continuous, non-stop, rolling snowball of projects, to-do's, tasks, and demands.

Remember, I said I know you...I AM YOU.

Here's the truth: You...Are...AMAZING! The work you do is amazing. You are brilliant and innovative. The world is made better because of you. However, the work of your hands, the mission you serve, and the organization you lead...those are all secondary. The real gift and true treasure is YOU. All else will be for naught if you are not truly ok, authentically present, and holistically thriving in your public and private life.

I write this to remind you of what you already know. Nurturing you is not idle time. Do you even realize how many people get nourished from the well that is you? Untended wells do run dry. Your interior life matters more than your exterior life.

Roles, rank, and title change. Your heart, soul, and purpose - those are constant.

This writing is not rooted in judgement. It is rooted in love. It is rooted in a desire to see longevity in your quality of life and leadership.

Tough Skin, Soft Heart Truth

Tough Skin: There will always be a list, to-do's, pressures, and demands, but there is only one me. I will pause, make time, adjust priorities, and build boundaries that encourage me not to lose sight of myself in the midst of the work.

Soft Heart: Sometimes the best answer to a busy day is to begin by practicing silence, solitude, personal reflection, and self-care.

Day 3
Learning to Leave the Table

"You've got to learn to leave the table when love's no longer being served."

— Nina Simone

Prolific artist, activist, and musician Nina Simone, known for her poignant and justice-laced lyrics, hit the nail on the head with this power truth. When we experience unrelenting toxicity in relationships, why do we stay? Why do we hunker down with people and root ourselves in places that continually hurt and injure us?

I can't judge. There have been times where I stayed in toxic work environments and perpetually wounding relationships much too long. We all know what it's like to remain in a place where love is not only gone, but even thinking love used to reside there seems comical. As I look over my life, my 20's are a blur because I stayed in leadership roles and spaces too long out of fear of disappointing other people, fear of failure, fear of speaking truth to power, and fear of retribution.

When you stay in a place where love used to be and now is gone, it is like a baby staying in prenatal incubation beyond the appointed time. What used to be the womb can quickly become a tomb. The same place that once served as an incubator of support and life can easily become your burial site. Are you inflicting pain upon yourself because you keep trying to resurrect love from a now defunct and dry place?

One weekend, a friend sent me a series of emails. She was battling injustice in the workplace and the battle was wrought with years and layers of dispute resolution, legal investigations, allegations, power dynamics, and distrust. She was writing to ask my advice and support as she prepared to launch another assault against a system that seemed stacked against her. She had hunkered down in this toxic space, becoming so encumbered in her pain and anger that she couldn't even see the true root cause of her anguish. The pain from her job was consuming her life, conversation, and relationships. The toxicity was spreading to every aspect of her identity. As I crafted a message in support of her, I didn't address the job. I asked her two questions: "With the fight you have left in the midst of such pain and anguish, is the best focal point, retaliation? Could you better use your energy on your own restoration?"

Our words about our work life can be such critical indicators of the toxicity of the environment. No work environment is perfect. As long as human beings exist and gather, fallibility will always be present. But there are work environments that become completely toxic to you and your well-being. It is hard to thrive, focus, and be well in a place where hurt is cyclical and the norm. Sometimes the best way to ignite the restorative process is with the sound of your feet leaving tables where love is no longer being served.

Tough Skin, Soft Heart Truth

Tough Skin: I will take inventory of the toxicity in my life. Are there areas of my own character, personality, and attitude that I need to change? Could these internal changes help yield the external changes I desire to see? Are there relationships and settings in my life that have become toxic? Am I on an overextended stay in a toxic environment?

Soft Heart: I will connect with sound, wise counsel within my inner circle to help me assess the toxicity in my life. I will be open to the honest feedback of those who love me and know me best. I will not languish in dead spaces by trying to resurrect love where it is no longer being served.

Day 4
Want it Without
the Work

My Truth: There are areas in my life where I want the results without the work. I want the successful outcome with little to no sweat equity. I want the flash, the lights, and the "Get it Girl" moment without the grunt work, labor, delayed gratification, or the climb. I want it yesterday, I want it now, I want it suddenly, and I want it with excellence. Remember the old Rice Krispy treat commercials? I want the "flour on my face" effect that comes from homemade baking. I just want the effect with the ease of opening a box of prepackaged treats.

News flash: I am not alone. We are in the same boat together. Maybe the easy wins that we want are different, but we all have areas in our lives where we crave the outcome of doing the work, without the pain of putting in the real work.

Now that our mutual truth is laid out, what do we do? Here's what we know:

1. Real change requires investment, effort, and work

2. Real change isn't at the finish line, it's occurring with each progressive step.

3. Real change is an "as you go" phenomenon

4. Real change isn't fast and requires deliberateness and intentionality.

What does this all mean?

We have to stop glamorizing the finish line and become journey-minded and step-oriented. Real and lasting change requires valuing every second, minute, hour, and baby step made in the right direction. It means a long-haul focus versus instant gratification. This type of change means struggle. It means dying to the habits, mindsets, and behaviors that have us longing for change in the first place. It means patience to stay the course and resistance to falling back or falling away. It means pressing toward the mark. It means understanding that real change always begins within before the fruit will bear externally.

Tough Skin, Soft Heart Truth

Tough Skin: I will focus less on the finish line. I will direct my energy towards consistent progress and staying the course.

Soft Heart: I will keep stepping in the direction of the change I want to see. It's happening as I go!

Day 5
Tears, Fears, and Leadership Behind the Veil

LEADERS CRY. I'm not talking about tears shed from an introspective reflection on the importance of the work you do. I'm not talking about the 'watery glisten' of unshed tears as a result of an unexpected honor, recognition, or random act of kindness. I'm not referring to tears of joy. I'm talking about the 'ugly cry' tears amazing leaders everywhere shed in parked cars and behind closed doors.

Leaders cry because they experience rejection, despair, and unmerited detractors from the most unwarranted spaces. Leaders cry because the dream isn't happening fast enough and because teammates sometimes morph into enemies. Leaders cry because the stress gets all-consuming and overwhelming. Leaders cry because the road gets rough and the way gets fog-filled with doubt, insecurity, loss, tragedy, loneliness, and scarcity. Leaders cry under the weight of the sacrifice and burden of the spotlight. Leaders cry out of their own pain. Leaders cry because darkness comes, light is elusive, and motion is still required. Leaders cry because efforts don't always manifest into desired movement and momentum. Leaders cry because they miss the days of being a follower with minimal responsibility. Leaders cry because sometimes the pain needs a place to go.

We cry because we are ordinary human beings seeking to use our lives, gifts, and voice to pursue the extraordinary. Simply put, leaders cry because that's what human folks do. We are hardwired to cry. Crying is not an operations malfunction, sign of weakness, lack of strength, or expression of frailty. Yet, as leaders, we are told we cannot cry. All too often, it is unsafe to cry. It is a misconception to believe that people who skillfully handle the stress of leadership never cry. Tears come because we have tear ducts, just like sweat comes because we have sweat glands. Tears are a biological cooling function to keep our heads and hearts from overheating and self-combusting. Tears are a natural release valve. Tears are indicators...built-in detection systems that inform us when something is awry and amiss.

The real conundrum is not if leaders should cry or why leaders cry. The better question is, "What now?" What action will you be motivated to take on the other side of a good cry? The answer to that question is the true pendulum space and significant moment.

The other day I watched a tennis match featuring an emerging star who had one set to win in order to defeat her challenger. For two hours, she had played under intense sun and audience scrutiny. The weight of the moment and a missed shot got to her. Cameras zoomed in as she swiped at a lone tear that fell from her eyes. She did a little self-talk, but soon that one lone tear evolved into a state of silent weeping. It was clear that the strain of the moment and pressure of competition was getting to her. The commentators made a fuss over the presence of tears. I sat watching and waiting for her post-cry response. See, tears often create a flight-or-fight space. In that moment, the tears could've been the release she needed to unleash an inalienable resolve to finish strong. In this case, the tears disrupted her focus, unhinged her confidence, and she lost.

Leaders need safe spaces to cry. Stop debating whether or not you should cry. As long as we are human, we WILL cry. The real question is what will we do on the other side of the tears we shed? Here's to using our tears as a reminder to check in with ourselves, gauge where we are, identify what we need, regroup, and refocus.

Tough Skin, Soft Heart Truth

Tough Skin: Crying is not an operations malfunction, sign of weakness, lack of strength, or expression of frailty. I will not ignore or be led by my emotions.

Soft Heart: Tears are a biological cooling function to keep our heads and hearts from overheating and self-combusting. Are there emotional indicators I've been suppressing that need attention?

Day 6
The Power of
Our Broken Places

"Shannon, I need 15 minutes to cry. I know we need to meet, but can I have 15 minutes, right here, right now...to cry?"

It was a Fall afternoon, and my client had just arrived at our crowded lunch spot for a project management meeting. Even without words, her whole visage told a story of unspoken despair, sadness, and stress. I turned the printed meeting agenda face down, and gently placed my hand on top of hers as she silently wept. I sat quiet as she released the tears that had been locked tight behind a mask of "I'm fine". For the past 48 hours she had worked tirelessly to assure her board, staff, and key stakeholders of financial comeback in the midst of dealing with a real and very-present setback. Earlier that week, she had received notice that a grant the organization had routinely received for years - a grant that supported 1/4 of her organization's workforce, was abruptly terminated. No time to process the shock, she had spent the first 48 hours in firefighter mode. Her days and nights had been full of meetings confronting implicit accusations, crafting emails to address internal fears, and worrying about the staff and families that would critically be affected if a solution to replace the lost dollars was not unearthed.

That fateful day became a defining moment for both of us. As she cried, I turned introspective about the challenges brewing in my own life. I started reflecting on the uncertainties and issues looming beneath my smile and mask of "I'm fine." In that moment, I affirmed what I had known for some time. It was time to pivot and shift #ToughSkinSoftHeart from a hobby/side hustle, into a calling I would pursue full-time. As her tears subsided, I grabbed napkins and together we mapped strategy. We went into a war room space of navigating a plan for her self-care and the organization's bounce back. She left our meeting, implemented the strategy we created, and raised 1.8x's more money than the grant that had been lost. Every time I think about that pivotal day, I am reminded of the **power of broken places.**

Some of our best ideas, businesses, leadership, and power moves emerge out of our broken places. Some of our greatest opportunities to impact arise from our 'woe is me' moments. The best beauty often arises from our ashes. In our pain, we find the wisdom to guide our progress. Like elders in my life often remind me...every promised land is preceded by a wilderness encounter.

As you review the game film of your life—what wisdom can you extract from your professional missteps? What pivotal lessons have you gleaned from the difficult seasons in your life and leadership? How can you wield the challenges you have faced and overcome to add to your competitive advantage in the marketplace?

Tough Skin, Soft Heart Truth

Tough Skin: There is power in my broken places! I will revisit the battles I have won and the challenges I have overcome to draw wisdom for the issues facing me today.

Soft Heart: The mantle of leadership gets heavy, but I don't have to bear the weight alone. Even in crisis, I will not be afraid or ashamed to reach out for the support I need.

Day 7
Bring the Calm

When others depend on us to lead and to serve, we can't afford to start our day without built-in time for our own wellness. We must have a few sacred space moments in the beginning of our day, unplugged from technology, with a chance to be nobody before being the rock to everybody. Starting our day from a place of self-care strategically positions us to bring the calm into our spaces of leadership.

A friend of mine posted a Swedish proverb on her Facebook page that I absolutely love. "The afternoon knows what the morning never suspected." Everyday people depend on us to be fire fighters, fire preventers, and in some cases, fire starters. Chaotic moments will arise in the day; the greatest asset we can offer in the midst of chaos is calm. In order to bring calm, we need to protect and create space for fostering our own peace.

For me, this means getting up earlier than anyone else in my house so I have time to just...be. I call it my 'cool of the day' time. In that time, I refuse to pick up my cell phone, laptop, or turn on the TV. I love lighting candles in my cool of the day time, going for walks outside, staring out the window at the trees, listening to music, praying, and even sitting in silence. This hour of intention helps me prepare for the day ahead and the demands that will arise.

Remember, how we show up is just as important as what we do once we show up. In order to show up strong, we have to make time to pour into ourselves before we get caught up in the pressures and demands of a life committed to being a difference maker.

Today's Tough Skin, Soft Heart Truth

Tough Skin: Being good to others starts with being good to myself. I can't give out what I don't have. I will fill my own reservoir of strength by taking time at the onset of each day to have my own quiet time.

Soft Heart: I will create an atmosphere that nurtures my calm so I can bring calmness to chaos today. I will slow down and be slow to speak, quick to listen, slow to anger, and quick to forgive. I will nurture calm from the inside-out so I can be a source of calm to stressful situations and the stressed-out people I encounter today.

Day 8

Is it Arson
or is it Fire?

Arson: Targeted, deliberate sabotage of a person, place, thing, group, or movement.

Leaders daily deal with pressure and fire situations. As leaders, we are constantly confronted with varying degrees of fire in relation to the people, initiatives, and organizations we serve and lead. Yet, sometimes challenges classified as fires are actually arson attempts. Arson is a fire intentionally ignited by a person[s]. Fires emerge spontaneously, but arson is masterminded with specific intent for nefarious purposes. Have you ever had a team member or subordinate withhold key information or deadlines from you, only to go public with the information when it's too late for you to act on it and the damage is done? Have you ever had a co-worker strategically use his or her knowledge and expertise to exploit your lack of knowledge or expertise in the same area? Have you ever had a colleague pledge private support, but use a public forum to speak ill of you, your work, or your vision?

Some arsonists love the thrill of drama and interpersonal conflict, others incite for retribution, and some arsonists even start fires out of sheer malice. Arsonists may leave a calling card; but most take painstaking effort to disguise an arson attempt as a spontaneous act of nature. Whether visible or invisible, and regardless of methodology or mode, arson at its root is the targeted, deliberate sabotage of a person, place, thing, or movement.

Default human behavior is to respond immediately to a fire. As leaders, we make haste to diffuse, contain, and resolve pressure situations that arise. However, arson is not your average fire; there is a human, professional, and fiscal price tag attached to how you handle it. Like grease fires, arson requires a different kind of fire-fighting strategy. Misdiagnosing a situation as fire instead of arson can lead to reactionary and impulsive decisions that feed right into the ultimate design of the arsonist.

As leaders, we must cultivate the wise practice of slowing down and taking time to dwell on a situation. Business etiquette denotes we respond to an email within 48 hours, but responding to an email doesn't mean acting or rendering a decision on a matter. Neglecting to take time to reflect and be strategic in response may result in throwing gasoline on the situation.

Here are some tips to help you navigate the next arson attempt you encounter:

Call 911 - Seek objective strategy support from trusted colleagues and mentors to skillfully diagnose and approach the situation. Calling '911' is especially helpful in times where arson attempts are marked and aimed at us, personally.

Turn off the heat source - Assess the root cause. As with grease fires, water is the worst thing to pursue as a solution to an arson fire. Arson attempts are best extinguished by cutting off the oxygen supply to the fire. In addressing arson attempts, stop to consider how to cut off the oxygen supply.

Practice consistent integrity and character—Arson is subversive and illegal. We need to stay in character and not use illegal fighting or underhanded tricks.

Avoid evacuating—Arson can be an attempt to uproot your leadership prematurely. Don't let an arson attempt short circuit your leadership longevity.

Today's Tough Skin, Soft Heart Truth

Tough Skin: The best-laid arson attempt is no match for a leader who responds from a place of wisdom. I will not allow pressure to move me to act or verbally respond with haste. I will slow down, assess the situations that confront me, and move forward in a manner that is strategic.

Soft Heart: Arson attempts arise for even the most seasoned of leaders. I will engage my circle of support to assist me in accurately diagnosing and developing strategic responses to the arson attempts confronting me. I will not allow the sabotage attempts of others to take me out of character in conversation, behavior, or demeanor.

Day 9
Rethinking Closed Doors: Today's Rejection = Tomorrow's Win

Our next great idea may spring on the heels of today's rejection.

The story of WhatsApp co-founder Brian Acton who sold his product to Facebook for $19 billion dollars enthralls me. Yes, you read that figure correctly...$19 BILLION DOLLARS!

While the sale itself is impressive, it is Acton's journey to this career high that I find riveting. In 2009, Brian Acton was a software engineer struggling to get hired.

Despite years of experience at Yahoo and other firms, Facebook and Twitter rejected him for employment. Yet, in five short years, he and a colleague partnered to develop WhatsApp, the world's largest global messaging company [at that time]. In 2014, Acton sold WhatsApp for $19 billion dollars to the same company that rejected him for a job. The sell price exceeded what was paid for Skype and Snapchat.

How do you turn a career low into a $19 billion dollar payday?

Acton's social media posts following those rejection experiences reveal valuable insights:

"Got denied by Twitter HQ. That's ok. Would have been a long commute."

- Brian Acton (@brianacton) May 23, 2009

"Facebook turned me down. It was a great opportunity to connect with some fantastic people. Looking forward to life's next adventure."

- Brian Acton (@brianacton) August 3, 2009

Acton embodied a post-rejection mindset echoed best by Richard Castle. "Rejection isn't failure. Failure is giving up. Everybody gets rejected. It's how you handle it that determines where you'll end up."

To pursue a vision or destiny that is bigger than us, we must be prepared to experience rejection. Remember this: The greatest innovation is often birthed on the heels of rejection.

Today's Tough Skin, Soft Heart Truth

Tough Skin: Somebody else's "no" is not powerful enough to derail my purpose unless I allow it to be. I will live in fearless pursuit of my dreams and the visions of my heart.

Soft Heart: Rejection stings, but the bigger sting would be to allow rejection to shut down my belief in my own brand, calling, and purpose. I will not internalize rejection and allow it to produce paralysis or fear in my life. I will be bold!

Day 10
"Can-Do" Folks Struggle with Asking for Help

Hearing a loud thud from the bathroom on one morning, I found my toddler standing silent in the middle of the floor with a look of concern, not knowing if he would be scolded or comforted. He had the look of good intentions gone awry. "Honey, what were you doing?" I asked.

"Brush teeth," he responded. Then it hit me. His potty doubled as a step stool. He was trying to mimic what he had seen me do every morning. In his attempt to pick up the step stool and move it to the sink to brush his teeth, he discovered it was too heavy and had dropped it.

We were on the verge of being late for our morning commute, but I knew this was a teachable moment I couldn't pass up. I leaned down, pulled him close and said, "Babe, it is okay to do some things on your own, but it is also okay to ask for help."

Like us, my son loves operating from a "can-do" space. As a toddler, he is very vocal about the things he can do unaided. He takes pride in his ability to mobilize and move without help. His newly discovered independence has emboldened him to try new things and test the boundaries of his aptitude. While his independence is to be celebrated and encouraged, there are moments and spaces where he, like us, requires help.

My spaces for help have grown more complex, but teaching my son held a boomerang lesson. Can-do folks struggle with asking for help. As leaders, we LOVE being helpful, but the plot thickens when we find ourselves in need of help. Just like my son, we know what it is like to flop, flounder, screw up, and injure ourselves (and others) because we did not ask for help.

Asking for help requires admitting a lack of knowledge, resources, capacity, or strength. Asking for help has to be prefaced by an honest acknowledgement of our limitations. To recognize that something is beyond our reach or that and we can't attain a desire unaided makes us vulnerable. Vulnerability is complex and often emotionally daunting.

Leaders like to be in control. It is hard enough to ask for help within our circles, but to need help in a way that moves us beyond our tribe or spaces of familiarity is even more difficult. Why? Most of us have learned the hard way that everyone is not a safe person to ask for help or to unveil our limitations to. Truth is, many of us have made such revelations only to have our vulnerability exploited, manipulated, or worse. Personality, culture, ethnicity/race, lived experiences, and childhood socialization add layers of complexity to our perceptions connected to needing and asking for help.

Sure, we know someone that is overextended, sick, and at the breaking point all because he or she refuses to ask for help. My experience with my son high-lighted spaces in my own life where I have learned truths in a "soft behind, hard head" way. What could've been averted and prevented in your life by asking for help? Are there situations escalating to a crisis in our lives because we have been too stubborn, proud, or fearful to cry out for help?

Today's Tough Skin, Soft Heart Truth

Tough Skin: Help is NOT a dirty word.

Soft Heart: Needing help is not a sign of weakness. Needing help is a human experience that transcends title, age, and years of experience. We can't truly thrive if we only find comfort in helping others. We can't afford to allow pride, past experience, and fear to prevent us from seeking out safe sources for help. Truth is, there are some spaces of greatness, wholeness, and victory we will never attain until we admit our need and ask for help.

Day 11
Talent + Character = A Good Name Matters

The 2016 United States' Presidential election cycle found both candidates under federal investigation for allegations of ethical violations. More than ever constructs of what makes an exceptional leader have expanded beyond talent and technical aptitude to include one's character. The world is full of talented and gifted people. The differentiator is character. Can your character sustain you in the places your networks and competencies take you? Do you honor your word? Is your behavior congruent with the values you espouse? Can your character speak for you even when you aren't in the room? Truth is: it does.

Our character precedes us, enters spaces long before our bodies do, and can even override professional acumen and dossier. Most of us have vetted another leader by inquiring about the person's ethics and integrity even before directly meeting or engaging the person ourselves. While there is intrinsic value in a good name, there is no such thing as a perfect name or mistake-free name. All of us miss it and fall short of self-imposed expectations and the expectations of others. Thankfully, character describes who a person is on a regular basis. We all know amazingly brilliant and credentialed folks who are a hot mess on the regular, mean-spirited as the norm, and cutthroat in practice.

Discussing the connection between talent and character is not a condemnation conversation; this is a growth and maturity conversation. The opportunities that emerge because of our gifts are best sustained by the application of character.

As a mentor once told me: technical competencies can be taught; but you inherit a person's character as is.

Today's Tough Skin, Soft Heart Truth

Tough Skin: Part of my personal and professional development plan must include ongoing work on my flaws, blind spots, and character. I choose to operate as a person of integrity within and outside of the spotlight.

Soft Heart: Technical competencies can be taught, but there is no substitute for character. Are there any aspects of my character that may be hindering growth opportunities in my life?

Day 12
We All Need
Truth-Tellers

Mutual accountability is the art of only asking of others what you are willing to require of yourself first. No wonder mutual accountability is such a buzzword in today's knowledge-based economy. Many modern-day practices like the 360 Performance Review, exit interviews, and flattened hierarchies all stem from increased workplace demands for greater accountability among all levels of leadership.

One of my mutual accountability partners is a truth-teller who doesn't shy away from difficult conversations and topics I would rather tiptoe around. She is a straight-shooter with an authentic desire to see me grow and win. As leaders, we need people in our lives who refuse to allow us to stay in dangerous spaces of avoidance, yet are mindful to remember that packaging matters. Skillful truth-tellers render well-seasoned words that "keep it real," but do not injure us. Leaders without mutual accountability partners run the risk of blind spots that can impede vision and success.

Here are a few qualities that I find indispensable in a mutual accountability partner.

Mutual Accountability Partners (MAPs)...

- Thrive with transparency—Positive change can't occur where honesty is absent. MAPs work best when both parties refuse to lie, omit, sugar coat, or pad the truth.

- Engage humility and grace—No matter how awesome we are, anyone who hangs around us long enough is bound to see and experience our flaws. MAPs extend grace because they understand the person who extends grace today will require grace tomorrow.

- Let it flow both ways—MAPs don't dish what they can't take. MAPs help each other own intention and impact.

- Have a "me too" mindset—MAPs are willing to look at their own flaws and shortcomings with the same intensity and critical eye used in identifying areas of growth in others.

Tough Skin, Soft Heart Truth

Tough Skin: Every leader experiences fatigue and blurred vision. I will use my circle of mutual accountability partners to help me "defrost" in foggy stretches of life and leadership.

Soft Heart: Mutual accountability is a strength-building strategy. I will pursue mutual accountability with colleagues and peers committed to seeing me win and grow as a difference maker.

Day 13
Leadership DNA

Evolving as leaders doesn't mean losing the old-school principles that shaped us. There is a difference between living in the past and being motivated by our past. Nostalgia is not always a bad thing. We each have leadership roots that anchor us and have strategically supported our trajectory from where we were to where we wanted to be.

Think about it: Some of our most skillful leadership tactics, abilities, and lessons in resilience were seeded long before any advanced education or fancy job title. We've all attended workshops, seminars, and conferences designed to hone our skills, but for many of us, the roots of our leadership ideology and values stem from adolescence. These foundational worldviews stem from our origin stories and serve as the DNA threads of our leadership. This leadership DNA sharpens with age and gets seasoned with experience, but the essence remains the same. It is important that, while our leadership evolves, we don't lose sight of the old-school principles that define and anchor us even today.

I am a native daughter of the city of Detroit. I grew up on the eastside of the city, and I still embody life lessons and principles gleaned from my beloved community and childhood experiences. Here are a few 'throwback' lessons embedded in my leadership DNA that still guide me today.

Lesson #1: Staying cutting edge professionally and on my "A" game begins with me and the habits I practice behind closed doors.

Right inside the front door of my childhood home was a coat closet with a large mirror on the front. Daily, I would stand in front of that mirror and, with a hair brush as a microphone, sing, talk to myself, and host a talk show featuring my sisters. In front of that mirror, I learned the power of my own voice. Since then, I've used many mirrors to perfect the art of oratorical speaking, self-encouragement, and being prepared. I've been through Toastmasters and attended other forums and facilitation trainings, but I still "kick it old school" and practice important presentations in front of the mirror.

Lesson #2: Communities Matter. Shared destiny is about seeing my story and life inextricably linked to all who call my community home.

One summer, I watched my dad stand in our driveway and negotiate with a 17-year old leader of a local moped crew. The teen leader and his crew were in our driveway preparing to confront our next-door neighbor's sons. My neighbor's sons were culprits in a series of home invasions in our community. One of the victims included the grandmother of the crew leader. The two sons had broken into his 70-year old grandmother's home and stole electronics, jewelry, cash, and precious artifacts belonging to his deceased grandfather. Street justice demanded recompense.

I watched my dad listen to and engage this group of 14- to 19-year-old youth. I watched him respect their code and culture while challenging them to rethink their style of pursuing honor and justice. I also watched my dad challenge the culprits to rethink stealing as a means of advancing economically. While other neighbors watched from their porches or behind blinds, my dad boldly stepped in to diffuse the situation and foster reconciliation. My childhood home became known in the community as a gathering hub and safe harbor for dealing with issues and crises in our neighborhood.

My professional career in community engagement and mobilization stems from lessons I learned while watching my parents and grandparents serve in our neighborhood and city. My earliest training in what it means to be a public servant and difference maker came from their living examples of leadership. I was taught the importance of addressing community ills from a space of listening, living among those you serve, mutual investment, and shared destiny. These lessons continue to guide how I think and operate as a leader today.

Lesson #3: Anyone can be a philanthropist. Everyone has something to give.

A woman from our church and her two daughters came to live with us when I was seven years old. The woman was exiting a marital relationship that had become physically abusive. My mother sang in the church choir with the woman and opened our 750-sq. ft. home to her and her family. My mom was a divorced, working mom of two young girls and had limited means. Yet, a week after learning of our church member's need, my mother invited her and her children into our tiny house. For a year they lived with us and my mom never asked for a dime. The woman went on to find employment and thrive. The modern housing movement today would call what my mom did the "housing first model." I call it "kicking it old school." In that home, I learned the quiet, unassuming power of service and faith in motion. Long before I would learn the clinical concepts of altruism and philanthropy, my mother exhibited the spirit of neighbor helping neighbor.

Tough Skin, Soft Heart Truth

Tough Skin: I am a product of the "old school." I will go back into the arsenals of my leadership DNA to draw strength and wisdom for the challenges I face today.

Soft Heart: My past is a testament archiving the peaks, valleys, lessons, and anchors that inform my leadership even today. I will draw richly from my past, carry the wisdom of my elders, and transfer my leadership DNA to the next generation.

Day 14
Pitchers and Bowls

Days when we're riding high on wins in our lives are perfect moments to stop, pray for, and give thanks to the people who relentlessly support us. Unexpected "I love you" or "I appreciate you" acts of kindness and words of affection ensure that we leave no place for unsung heroes in our lives. Making time for recognition and gratitude is critical. Wise leaders embed gratitude and recognition as a culture and lifestyle practice versus sporadic occurrence.

Truth is, all of us need to give and receive recognition and gratitude. Everyone vacillates between seasons of strong and weak; being a mentor and being the mentee. Like my friend Tarra says, "We have to be pitchers and bowls in each other's lives." Pitchers pour and make deposits. Bowls receive and hold what has been poured.

Let's take inventory: Who are the folks that act as pitchers in our life?

Who are the people that:

- Intentionally and routinely make deposits into our purpose, development, and dreams

- Stand in our corner both in dark moments and in the spotlight

- Were present before the world knew our name and have committed to being there even if the rest of the world walks out

- Firmly believe that when you win, they win

- Aren't afraid of our ascent nor absent in our demise

- Have used their backs, hearts, and hands to help us stand strong when our courage waned and gave out

Now, look at your list of names reflecting the people that are pitchers in your life. Make time consistently to honor and validate the folks on your list. Be present in their life not just as a bowl, but as a pitcher. Deposit into their dreams and souls. May we live not just as takers, but givers into the lives of those who bless and make our lives better!

Today's Tough Skin, Soft Heart Truth

Tough Skin: I didn't get here on my own. I will actively seek to be a blessing to those who have supported my journey. Today, I put myself in remembrance of all who have relentlessly sowed into my life, nurtured my passions, and believed in me.

Soft Heart: I will not allow myself to neglect or forget the hands and hearts that have contributed to the wins in my life. I will be proactive in rendering thanks and support to my inner circle. I will love, support, encourage, fund, and believe in them. They won't have to assume or imply how I feel. They will hear regularly how I feel from me. I will invest in the relationships and people that matter most.

Day 15
FADS

I love watching the television series *Project Runway*! Each episode, host Heidi Klum repeats her infamous mantra to the fashion designer contestants, "One day you're in, and the next day you're OUT."

Fashion isn't the only industry that operates that way. Nearly every industry has seasons of "what's hot and what's not." Today's industry superstar can be obscure and forgotten tomorrow. That's why, as leaders, it is so important to put praise from people in the proper perspective. If we are not mindful, we can all fall prey to selling our souls for the recognition of others only to lose sight of ourselves when the attention is gone.

Determine that you will exhibit the same character, integrity, service, and work ethic whether the light is on or off. Staying power and leadership longevity is about consistently being our best self, no matter who is watching and what is trending.

Tough Skin, Soft Heart Truth

Tough Skin: I will not sell out my values and beliefs for a short-lived spotlight. I am after longevity in my leadership. Praise may come and go, but my strength of character will stand the test of time.

Soft Heart: I want to receive praise and recognition for my accomplishments, but will not chase after or crave the spotlight to the point of self-compromise. I will not base my worth as a leader on who sings my praises or who fails to notice. My brand is anchored in my integrity, character, service, and ethic. Those traits never go out of style.

Day 16
Older, Wiser, Stronger

The other day, I:

- Took the scenic route to a meeting instead of the expressway.

- Got up early to prep my Crockpot so dinner would be ready when I got home

- Had my prayer and devotion time

- Practiced the art of being bold when needed and holding my peace when I should

The older I get, the more I value a holistic approach to leadership. Leading doesn't begin when I step into a room full of people. Leadership begins in my private life.

Nourishing my own soul, focusing on the essential, and taking care of home matters. My public life can't thrive for long if my internal well-being and personal life are a hot mess. My greatest work gains emerge on the other side of slowing down long enough to get me and my interior life in order. Only then can I show up with my best self wherever I go. The older, wiser, and stronger me understands that leadership longevity is rooted in the practice of leadership from the inside-out.

Today's Tough Skin, Soft Heart Truth

Tough Skin: I don't want to be high-functioning in the marketplace and unwell behind closed doors. I will address the "junk drawer" areas of my own life. I understand that my sustainability as a leader is inextricably connected to my personal state of affairs.

Soft Heart: I will not place a premium on my public life above my personal life. Being a conscious and connected leader requires that I be an excellent overseer of my own affairs first.

Day 17
What Do You Want?

If we never honestly ask and answer the question "What do I want," how can we truly live as captains of our own destinies?

As busy leaders, we are often consumed with activities that place a premium on outside expectations. Much of our time is dedicated to addressing what others need, want, and expect from us. Managing and meeting the expectations of others can become life-consuming, dream-altering, and purpose-draining.

Let's pause in this moment and consider the last time we asked, pondered, and answered the question: "What do I want?" There is no way to live at the intersection of joy and purpose without asking this fundamental question. I am not suggesting that we shift to the other end of the spectrum and become totally me-first and selfish. I am, however, elevating an idea that each of us needs to develop and act from a self-inclusive mindset.

Think of self-inclusive living like the air mask policy of major airlines. Doing good for others begins with being good to ourselves. Cultivating this mindset is about listening to and valuing the voice of our own soul. It's about respecting our value and our heart. Yes, there are times and seasons in our lives when operating at the intersection of "obligation and duty" or "need-to but don't-want-to" are required. We all know what those seasons of life and leadership are like.

Yet, more times than not, we truly do have opportunities to ask and hold true to the outcomes we desire. How might our lives be different if we better incorporated our own needs and voice as a decision-making litmus test? What if we measured every choice and action against whether or not the decision would move us closer to or away from the dreams and desires of our heart? Asking what we want helps clear, minimize, and eliminate the clutter of external voices.

Tough Skin, Soft Heart Truth

Tough Skin: Being a great leader is not always synonymous with placing myself last or never considering myself at all. I don't have to martyr my own needs and interests all the time. Sometimes invoking the best in others begins with invoking the best in me.

Soft Heart: It is not a sign of humility to never ask myself what I want or need. Taking inventory of my own heart is not an act of selfishness. In fact, if I better listen to my own voice, I can help others hear their voices.

Day 18
The Stranger

She prayed for me. She didn't know me. I didn't know her. Our paths had never crossed. She took a risk, to say "hi" and to compliment me on my smile and attire. Her kind words met me on a day when I was feeling down and unsure. She gently patted my hand; she brought a tenderness that suggested we were friends meeting up for tea, even though we were strangers connecting for the first time during the lunch hour in a crowded cafe.

She made time stand still. She was warm, inviting, and open. She somehow sensed something looming behind my smile and asked if she could pray for me. I closed my eyes. I sat, she stood. I listened, and she prayed. Her prayer sounded the cries I had echoed only hours earlier while driving in my car. The stranger prayed for increase in my life and business. She prayed for me. I struggled as tears found their way to the corners of my eyes. Her eyes opened and glistened. I later found out she and her husband were new pastors to the area. Where she worshipped didn't matter. On that day, she was the epitome of faith and kindness in motion. She sought me out and prayed for me on a day I struggled to pray for myself.

Sometimes our superpower as difference makers is the ability to step right into the sticky thicket of other folks' lives and situations.

To not be afraid to wade in, dive in, jump in, get mixed up, and help turn things right side up.

To connect and touch – not by email, or social media. To wrap our hands in the cradle of another.

To let people know they are not invisible, that we see them.

To make ourselves available to pause, sit, be still, hear, and support.

The woman who held my hand didn't know it, but I was on the grind, preparing for the second biggest launch of my vision. I was scared. Her prayer was therapy to the soul; she articulated what I had been struggling to say all day. She stepped out of her comfort zone and into my situation. I needed that. I needed to hear someone praying for me.

Tough Skin, Soft Heart Truth

Tough Skin: Boldness and vulnerability can open doors of opportunity and dialogue.

Soft Heart: I don't have to know you to be a blessing to you.

Day 19
Getting to the Grape

It was a Thursday morning and my son Deuce and I were running late. I was rushing to get us both out of the door in the midst of an arctic-blast winter day. I flitted around, warming up the car, packing my work bag, getting boots on, and trying to appear calm as if we had all the time in the world when we didn't. Deuce was hungry, unwilling to wait until he arrived at school to have breakfast. I put a few grapes in a plastic bag and handed them to my toddler to distract him while I returned to the busy morning preparations.

As we got in the car, I caught my son lifting the bag preparing to rip the bottom of the plastic bag with his teeth. "NO, NO honey! Why didn't you ask me to help you?" (As if he hadn't seen me running around the past 15 minutes in a mad dash.) He looked at me calmly, feeling no sense of alarm. In my mind, all I could hear was our family dentist warning against using his teeth as scissors. In Deuce's mind, he had simply come up with a direct way of getting to his grapes. In that brief moment, my son had used deductive reasoning to explore a new way to get the job done.

Sometimes as adults, we get so set in established rules and paradigms. At some point, these traditional ways of doing things get cemented as the right way and the only way. The danger in doing so is the loss of adaptability, flexibility, and innovation. Everyday life throws us curve balls. Adults approach curve balls spending too much time and energy lamenting the curve ball itself. Children have a much easier time shedding one plan for another. After all, the goal is to reach the end goal, not to reach the goal the same way every time.

There are times in life when we have to go rogue and use new techniques to deal with an issue. I'm not always going to be there to give my son help. Sure, he would have opened the bag through messier, unconventional means, but he wouldn't have gone hungry. Sometimes the resolution is more important than the method.

Tough Skin, Soft Heart Truth

Tough Skin: I will look at life through a child's eyes, reminding myself that:

a) Opportunities are endless. There are infinite ways to get to the end goal.

b) From play often comes the best ideas.

c) "No" is often the best motivation to spark a second attempt.

Soft Heart: I will slow down today and see if the unconventional solution I need is staring me in the face.

Day 20
We Are All Winners!

We are not winners because life is picture perfect. We're not winners simply because of degrees, career titles, accomplishments, or external stuff. We are winners because we are breathing. And if we are breathing, there is still time to get it right, get it together, get moving, get focused, get recharged, get connected, get it in, or let it go.

Each breath is a reminder of the limitless opportunities we have to make choices for the good of ourselves and others. So, breathe deep, and let's GO!

Tough Skin, Soft Heart Truth

Tough Skin: Accolades and titles come and go. I will not place my identity, worth, or value in external things that may be subject to change.

Soft Heart: How I see myself matters. Even though I am striving each day to grow, improve, and evolve, I will celebrate the wins that exist in my life today. I will not wait until I achieve some "future state" to celebrate and affirm who I am. My ability to win in life long-term is connected to being able to see myself as a winner today.

Day 21
No...I Will NOT
Adjust the Volume

Stifle [stīfəl]: To make someone unable to breathe properly, suffocate. Choke, drown, or smother.

Every day presents itself with people, situations, and circumstances that will attempt to shut down, smother, and suffocate our dreams, identity, voice, and right to exist. These microaggressions often peak in spaces and seasons of our lives where we have great opportunity to be transformational and to participate at a greater degree in our life calling and purpose.

Being stifled not only silences our voices. If unchecked, it can smother and shut down the power and greatness that is supposed to grow inside of us and radically impact the lives of others.

Let's commit to not turn down the volume on our purpose. Instead let's ramp up the sound of a radiant life and existence.

Tough Skin, Soft Heart Truth

Tough Skin: This is MY season, MY time, and MY moment is NOW. I will operate in boldness and fearlessly enter every space as my authentic self. I will not allow the opinions, likes, or dislikes of others to mute my existence, voice, and dreams.

Soft Heart: Doing what I LOVE is motivation and affirmation enough. I won't spend another second of my life waiting for others to approve before I act, agree before I do, or like before I move.

Day 22
Reclaim Your Superpower

I tried to cut it off, ignore it, and subdue it. I tried to snuff it out, reason it away, and even pray it gone. I tried to be someone else, copy other people, and act like it wasn't so. Truth is, we all have.

We all have some innate personality traits and gifts that we don't always love. How much time have you spent in a love-hate relationship with some aspect of your identity or individual uniqueness. For me, I struggled with being the kid that always had an eye for people who felt left out or were visibly 'invisible'. I always had a keen eye for who was on the fringe, didn't fit, or didn't belong. Even when I was 'in', I was highly cognizant of who was out – of who wasn't invited to the party, who stood along the wall at the dance, who didn't get a love gram for Valentine's Day in high school. I could literally 'feel' the pain of people deemed outsiders, misfits, and labeled as the 'other'. Many times, I felt on the fringe of that myself, but my friendliness always seemed to land me just barely on the desirable side of cool.

What I loathed as a teenager, I have now embraced in my adulthood as my competitive advantage. Being a head+heart leader is a unique gift and an asset. What I used to deem a deficit, I have now come to appreciate as a strength and superpower! I would wager that some of the traits you have struggled to accept and validate about yourself may actually be gifts that position you to be transformative in the lives of others. What are your superpowers and how will you use them today to be impactful in the spaces and places you give leadership to?

Today's Tough Skin, Soft Heart Truth

Tough Skin: I am impressive handiwork. I will appreciate, celebrate, and own all of the unique qualities that make me who I am.

Soft Heart: I will reflect on the areas I have possibly diagnosed incorrectly as deficiencies. I will explore with intentionality my own superpowers!

Day 23
The Pep Talk

Leaders have rough days, and each of us is at some point along the spectrum of conceiving, birthing, and scaling a dream.

We are leaders replete with blueprints for innovation, social change, entrepreneurship, and community, so we get weary. We experience days fraught with challenges that have us feeling defeated before our morning coffee has cooled. We experience seasons where the dream isn't happening fast enough, times when resources are scarce, and fleeting moments when even we, the visionaries, doubt and question. In these "dark before the dawn" moments, our vision gets blurry. As leaders, we need safe spaces to receive the pep talks we need in order to replenish our motivation, re-visualize our goals, and remain steadfast despite adversity.

Several months ago, while in a "dark before the dawn" moment, I wrote a pep talk to myself that I revisit often. It is my living reminder that defeat is not an option and quitting is not in my DNA. This pep talk has become my go-to whenever I lose sight and the vision gets blurry. I call this anthem "When."

WHEN

When people call me crazy...I'm still   doing it

When the applause goes silent...I'm still doing it

With tears in my eyes...I'm still doing it

Despite intermittent bouts of self-doubt ...I'm still doing it

When fear strikes...I'm still doing it

Tough Skin, Soft Heart

When detractors lurk and attack... I'm still doing it

Before the world knows my name...I'm still doing it

When my heart struggles to believe...I'm still doing it

When the dream is nigh, but resources are slim...I'm still doing it

When a party of one...I'm still doing it

In the infancy stage...I'm still doing it

Post failure and loss...I'm still doing it

Through the pain...I'm still doing it

Whether others believe or not...I'm still doing it

No matter who is on board...I'm still doing it

When it seems like the dream will never materialize...I'm still doing it

When fatigue clouds my vision...I'm still doing it

When I feel alone...I'm still doing it

When I'm feeling strong...I'm still doing it

When the odds are stacked...I'm still doing it

When victory is a long shot...I'm still doing it

When I lose hope...I'm still doing it

When I feel inadequate...I'm still doing it

When my work is invisible...I'm still doing it

When my work is heralded...I'm still doing it

Despite changes in scenery, supporters, and situations...I'm still doing it

With or without fame...I'm still doing it

When battle is at its highest...I'm still doing it

When I struggle with contentment... I'm still doing it

My drive to continue is not rooted in the praise of people, what I possess, or what I go through. The calling on my life is unstoppable, without repentance, and irrevocable by self or man. It is longstanding, withstanding, enduring, invincible, divinely given, inspired and empowered. This gift cannot be robbed, broken, or destroyed. My purpose cannot be killed or devoured. It is in the resilience of purpose—an unshakeable set of gifts to pursue a calling bigger than me—that I continue to stand and do, fight and soar, win and thrive. Even on my worst day, my purpose thrives. I will live to do it and die being able to say, it was done.

Shannon M. Cohen

Tough Skin, Soft Heart Truth

Tough Skin: My dream is not a matter of if, but one of when. I won't let my dream die undone.

Soft Heart: My life has meaning and is destined to have a reach that extends far beyond me. There are other people waiting for me to walk in the fullness of my talents and gifts. The world needs what is brewing on the inside of me.

Day 24
Why Leadership is Like Cooking in a Crockpot

There are issues that we as front line, C-Suite, executive leaders just DON'T broadcast. Our typical modus operandi is to wrestle behind closed doors, to keep our challenges on tacit and simultaneously present an "I'm fine" game face to the masses.

I went through an 'I'm fine' season. Outwardly, I appeared fine, but inwardly I was angry and dissatisfied about some career-related outcomes. Feelings of despair crowded my thoughts: "Why am I still here and not THERE? I'm putting in the work...WHEN will the fruit of my labor materialize?" I grew weary and impatient with the seed, time, and harvest process. I was in a microwave space of wanting a RIGHT NOW actualization of my efforts and dreams. I was going through the motions of meetings, proposals, and networking, but internally, I was out of steam with sowing and anxious for reaping. Before I knew it, despair showed up with its cousin, ingratitude. That valley season was an indelible reminder of the role process and time play in the life journey of leaders.

Here's what that season taught me:

Patience - Some moves can't be rushed and not everything is served instantly. Like my friends at Daddy Pete's BBQ say, "Some things need to cook low and slow." That valley space reminded me of the crockpot seasons of leadership. Ever touch the side of a Crock-Pot to ensure it was on? It is, but low and slow. Leadership can be like cooking in a Crock-Pot.

Consistency - Go to bed, get up, and do it again! Sometimes the hardest thing to do is remain constant in the midst of present-day circumstances. The winning strategy is often on the other side of staying the course!

Gratitude - There is an inextricable connection between gratitude and attitude. If not addressed, discontent and dissatisfaction can feel like walking around wearing soaking wet socks in dry shoes. Leadership is not a straight path, and anyone who says it is hasn't been a leader long. Leadership is full of detours and silent seasons, growth and triumph, invisible highs and lows. Gratitude is what keeps us from uprooting the seeds we have planted before the germination process is complete. Waiting time always precedes harvest. I am learning to not become so achievement driven that I forget to be thankful in and for the process.

We can't expedite purpose nor rush destiny. How might returning to a focus on patience, consistency, and gratitude help to disrupt the discontent soundtrack that may be on repeat in the jukebox of your soul?

Tough Skin, Soft Heart Truth

Tough Skin: I will be content as I wait for my next season of life and leadership. I will not rush the process or show up before I am ready. I will not wait until I can see with my eyes the architectural designs of my heart. I am thankful and content now.

Soft Heart: In everything, I give thanks. Gratitude is a natural heat check for my attitude.

Day 25
Get Louder

I remember when our son turned one year old. It was fascinating watching him grow increasingly verbal with each passing day. He loved waving and saying "Hi" to people, especially when we went shopping. It was during one of those grocery store excursions that my son had his first encounter with rejection. My son, being his bubbly 12-month old self, waved exuberantly to a gentleman in the aisle with us and said, "Hello." Stranger: no response. My son paused; He elevated his volume and waved enthusiastically. No response. I watched the exchange trying not to assume the worst about the stranger's blatant rejection of my son's fervent gesture of kindness. Then the most interesting thing happened, the more the man ignored my son, the LOUDER his greeting of hello became! In the face of this man attempting to render my son invisible, my child didn't shrink. He made the man uncomfortable by growing increasingly more targeted in his approach.

Watching my son made me wonder how many times I have allowed someone's lack of acknowledgement, disapproval, rejection, or blatant meanness to shut me down and cause me to cower in response.

Rejection takes many forms:

- Having our idea dismissed, tabled, or overruled

- Being excluded from a decision-making table

- Having our credentials and expertise questioned

- Being passed over for promotion or opportunity for advancement

- Having our kindness unreciprocated

Whether our recent rejection encounters have been explicit or implicit, overt or covert - we should take a lesson from my son's handbook of human interaction and refuse to allow a "no" to shut us down.

Tough Skin, Soft Heart Truth

Tough Skin: I will not allow a misplaced "no" to shut down me down, especially when it comes to my personality, dreams, or purpose.

Soft Heart: A "yes" from my lips to my ears and heart are stronger than any "no" or rejection response from another.

Day 26
OUCH!

Ever stubbed a toe? No matter our age, a stubbed toe can cause a full body shut down. Every pain receptor, nerve ending, and thought immediately shifts to the recoiling pain we feel in that itty-bitty, teeny-tiny part of our body. Stubbing a toe will cause us to forget where we are walking to and what we needed to do. Pain will cause our bodies to DEMAND a response. Pain can shut down our focus and cause time itself to stand still.

That's just physical pain. Now, imagine the impact of pain of the heart. Emotional pain is just as poignant as physical pain. Yet, stigma and shame prevent so many of us from admitting to and seeking treatment for non-physical pain. We live in a culture where living with chronic pain is normalized. We are implicitly taught to live with pain. We talk about managing pain, dulling the pain, enduring the pain, or waiting the pain out. These concepts may work with physical pain, but can wreak havoc on our souls.

I wonder if our present state of affairs of "walking wounded" is a result of our threshold for pain being too high. Have we somehow made it noble to silently suffer through pain rather than remove ourselves from harm's way?

I am not suggesting a swing to either end of the continuum. Life is not a bed of roses. Life is not unending sunny days. Hurtful experiences are a part of the human experience just like stubbed toes are a part of life. But sometimes we suffer in ways we don't have to.

Tough Skin, Soft Heart Truth

Tough Skin: Ouch! Life hurts! Pain is part of the human experience just like stubbed toes are a part of life, but I do have a say in how I respond. I am not powerless. I will not subsist in chronic hurt and pain when I don't have to.

Soft Heart: It is hard to focus when all of my energy is being used to protect myself. I will not allow stigma, shame, lack of resources, embarrassment, or fear to prevent me from getting the emotional, mental, and spiritual wellness support I need. I will take steps daily towards my own health and wholeness.

Day 27
Diagnosis --
Hearing Loss

It's funny what happens when we take time to be alone with ourselves. No TV or technological devices, no distractions or noise, just silent reflection. I was in a space like that recently. I was alone with my thoughts, my issues, my dreams, my breath, feeling in tune to my heart and soul. In that space of quiet reflection, I began to think about a leap of faith I needed to take and thought about the danger of safety nets.

At first glance, safety nets seem harmless...prudent even. Yet, there are times in each of our lives when the fearless pursuit of purpose requires burning our safety nets.

For many of us, safety nets have become our response to a hidden nemesis: doubt. Self-doubt is a natural knee-jerk response experienced on the precipice of something great. When we prepare to enact a vision, dream, or initiative that is bigger than us, we should expect doubt to surface.

Doubt, just like faith, can be fed and nurtured or starved and neglected. As I sat snuggled in my blanket that morning, I realized that pursuing the dreams of my heart would require jettisoning doubt and becoming more vigilant about who and what I listen to. It was time to practice self-imposed hearing loss. Self-imposed hearing loss is about refusing to give leverage to people, thoughts or things that shut us down, cause us to spiral into negative spaces, or paralyze us from forward movement. Our ears are access points, receptors, and gateways to our soul. We must be mindful of what we let in.

Tough Skin, Soft Heart Truth

Tough Skin: I won't allow doubt to ensnare me in safety nets constructed out of fear. I will protect the dreams I am working on by practicing intentional and filtered listening.

Soft Heart: I recognize that my ears are a command post for warding off words that could contaminate the vision of my heart. My dreams will be hard enough to fight for without entertaining doubt fueled by other people. I am done with small thinking. I will mute people, thoughts, and things that shut me down, cause me to spiral into negative spaces, prevent me from forward movement, or inhibit the transition of my dreams from ideation to implementation.

Day 28
Private Conversation vs Public Confrontation

We live in a day and age where technology, instead of direct contact, is used to voice displeasure.

Back in the day, when we received poor customer service, we would have to mail or email a letter to management expressing our dissatisfaction. Writing made it easy for concerns to go unnoticed. However, with the advent of social media and consumer-driven sites like *Yelp, Angie's List, TripAdvisor*, etc. consumer voice can obliterate a company's brand in 140 characters or fewer. The onset of rapid response technology has placed influence in the hands of the consumer. Businesses, in turn, respond less to address the wrong and more to avoid public shame.

This marketplace trend has crossed over into interpersonal conflict management and we have seen it wreak havoc on relationships. We have seen a rise in disagreements playing out over media via text messages, *YouTube* videos, *Facebook* posts, *Twitter* rants, and comment sections of blogs. Technology gives the boldness of anonymity; we are much more apt to say things online that we would never say in the same way, with the same intensity, or, at all, in person. The problem is we are losing the art and etiquette of having difficult conversations. Private conversations for dispute resolution have been replaced with public confrontation.

A few years ago, I facilitated a conflict resolution workshop for a nonprofit organization. As the session progressed, I watched a member of the management team move from struggling to hold back tears to silently weeping. As part of the presentation, I asked each team member to revisit a recent conflict, reflect on how they handled the situation, and share lessons learned from the experience. The woman who had been crying raised her hand and shared a story about receiving an upsetting text message from a close friend. Via text, the friend confronted her about allegations she heard from a third party. Her friend was told by the third party that the now weeping woman was going around saying that she didn't want the longtime friend in her life anymore.

The woman was teary as she shared how hurtful the text had been and how hard it was for her to understand why the friend believed the third party. What about all they had gone through? The ups and downs they had supported one another through? The sisterhood forged between them after the death of their parents? She was distressed that her friend would reject an opportunity to call or meet in person to talk, and rely on text messaging to confront such a delicate situation.

Technology is no substitute for face-to-face connections. Could a misunderstanding be avoided by stopping by a colleague's office instead of sending an email? Could a conflict be diffused by connecting to talk at a local coffee shop instead of by text?

Tough Skin, Soft Heart Truth

Tough Skin: I will use face-to-face conflict fluency strategies instead of relying on technology. I won't use humiliation, embarrassment or shame as techniques to win an argument.

Soft Heart: Even in my anger and frustration, I will humanize the person whose behavior or words have injured me. Tomorrow, it may be my behavior or words that prove injurious to someone else, and I will need to be on the receiving end of someone humanizing me.

Day 29
The World Won't Get My Best

We expend so much of ourselves during the workday. Our schedules are replete with meetings, navigating problems, and balancing so many demands. By the time we land home, the weight of the day can cause our brains to switch to silent or airplane mode. For many of us, our post-work commute home provides the first opportunity to since leaving for work to be still, silent, and a bit unplugged. While we want to see our families and significant others, it is sometimes with the unspoken disclaimer of: can we not use words please?

Even in the midst of our post-workday fatigue, my husband and I have a mantra that became cemented with the arrival of our son: we will not give the world our best smiles, hellos, and manners, only to come home and treat each other like leftovers.

I know that at the end of the day, no one has my back, best interest, or holds my heart like my husband does. I have determined that no matter where my purpose or career take me, I will not come home in a dry, foul, dead-woman-walking space to him or my son. I will not allow the fatigue of the day to cause me to respond to my family with short and snarky comments. I keep a special reservoir just for them.

Sometimes I have to retreat internally for a minute to shake off the day, before I tune into family life. In this day and age where our phones ping at all times of night, where email management feels like a part-time job, and work and home life boundaries feel drawn in water, we must vigilantly carve

136

out undivided time and attention for those who matter most.

I love and collect fine china. I am learning the importance and power of pulling out my best china for my loved ones — not just for company. Just like my china, the best of my attitude won't solely be for clients and colleagues. We can easily take family members for granted and expect them to understand why we're cranky, why we don't want to talk, why we're irritated, or why we're drowning the last of our day in front of the TV. The interesting thing is, even when we feel drained, many of us still find time to surf social media sites or power up computers and email to get a head start on the headaches of tomorrow.

I never hear anyone say at the time of death, "I wish I had returned more emails. I wish I had done more reports." I do hear people regret relationships. Save your good stuff. Do whatever it takes to tap into it.

Laugh, smile, giggle, dance, play music. Take the long route home so you can get into the proper mental space to greet, see, serve, and spend time with those that matter most.

Tough Skin, Soft Heart Truth

Tough Skin: By the world's standards, I am replaceable. To my loved ones, I am the world. I won't give those that deem me replaceable the choicest parts of my essence, attention, time, or commitment.

Soft Heart: I will develop my own 'unplug' policy and ritual to help me disconnect from the world of work and reconnect with the people and things that matter most. My job will not claim my life. My passion and those I love will get the prime spot!

Day 30
Breaking Point

FACT: Leaders experience breaking points. A breaking point is a moment or season of anguish due to the weight and pressure of a difficult situation.

<u>I've discovered a few truths about breaking points:</u>

- A breaking point is part of leadership boot camp. We can't just lead during the sunshine. Typhoon seasons require leadership too!

- Breaking points bring uncertainty and stir up fear of failure.

- There is no shame in being at a breaking point.

- When we are at breaking point, we have to invite the help and support of people we can trust.

- With trusted support, we can navigate the emotional aspects of a breaking point and develop our strategy.

- Quiet time and unplugging will help us recharge following a breaking point.

- Difficulty is a learning lab space. What we learn in this experience will prepare us for the next level.

- We are tough and resilient.

- Breaking points don't last forever. There is calm after the storm.

Tough Skin, Soft Heart Truth

Tough Skin: The classrooms that help groom me for greatness may not look like classrooms. Sometimes these places of learning and growth show up as pain, rejection, isolation, and difficulty. What can I learn in this difficult space? How might this space help me to develop the resilience I will need for life at the next level?

Soft Heart: I don't have to be an island just because I am in a difficult life and leadership place. Friends, loved ones, mentors, sponsors, coaches, allies, and advocates care about me and would love to walk alongside me. I will seek out trusted members of my tribe who can be there for me emotionally and professionally. I will not be afraid to be vulnerable and transparent.

Day 31
Twelve Months
in Review

What major life lessons and personal growth moments have the past 12 months revealed in your life? Here are my 12 months in review.

January –Sometimes we have to leap and not look down. January taught me how to leap, jump, and soar. You cannot live at the intersection of joy and purpose without taking some giant leaps!

February—February reminded me that dreams don't build themselves. As dreamers, we must get to a place of no longer apologizing or seeking permission before walking in the fullness of who we are.

March—I came out of the winter season with some "I Am" reminders: I am Resilient. I am Purpose-Driven. I am Enough. Thanks March!

April—Spring was a season of learning that moving forward often requires taking steps without a preview of the final outcome. I was re-acquainted with the power and necessity of faith.

May—The planting season reminded me that real success starts underground, out of public view. In this reality media age, it is so easy to spend all of our time inhaling others' reality and watching their life unfold while our dreams idle on the back burner. I started seeing my time as valuable currency and rerouting free-time activities to support my goals.

June—With great visibility comes great scrutiny. The summer was a blatant reminder that as a leader, I live under a magnifying lens and microscope. The sun that lights me, also exposes me.

July—Just because I am going through fire doesn't mean I have to smell like smoke. Summer was hot, but I stayed relentless. I did not allow the heat of life's challenges to redefine my character.

August—August reintroduced me to the notion of frenemies. The more our light shines, the more heat or opposition we may attract. Shine no matter what!

September—We all miss it...even on days full of our best intentions to get it right. September showed me my humanity. I will carry into the new year an intentionality to extend grace when facing the flaws of others; I need grace when folks encounter mine.

October—Girl, you have greatness in your bones! The advent of Fall was a season of personal affirmation. I was never made to live small.

November—November had one central question: How will I invest 30 minutes a day in pursuit of at least one dream? Time ain't slowing down and my plate will always be loaded, but if I can't sow 30 minutes of my own time into my own life and purpose...I have a problem.

December—Leadership is about expenditure. Each day people and things make withdrawals on our time, expertise, energy, and soul. Just like automobiles and bank accounts, withdrawals with no deposits leave leaders in a dry place and on "Empty." Left unattended, this will begin showing up in our external brand, zeal, health, etc. December reminded me of two things: [1] No matter how busy I am, I make time for what I truly want to do. I can find a way to make time for self-care. [2] Without proper fuel, I don't run well.

Tough Skin, Soft Heart Truth

Tough Skin: Some stuff just has to go. There is no room in the new year for insecurities, inconsistencies, and immaturities of the past. I'm purging to pack light for the journey ahead.

Soft Heart: Some insecurities, inconsistencies, and immaturities may inevitably seep over into the new year, but that's okay. I will give myself the space and grace to tackle the areas of my life that still need to be made over. There is still time, and the battles I have overcome this year prove that I am capable and able.

Day 32 - Bonus
Doin' It in the Dark

In 2017, 26-year old Lucas Holliday went from obscurity to fame. By day, Lucas worked as a cashier at a Lansing, MI. based Dollar General. By night, he served as lead musician in a local band. At his cashier job, he made a practice of singing covers of hits made famous by his favorite R&B artists. Each work shift, he would sing to customers while he bagged their purchases. In 2017, a customer videotaped Lucas singing Maxwell's hit, *Ascension* and posted the video to her Instagram page. Within hours, Lucas' powerful acapella cover went viral with millions of views, likes, and shares! Within days, the artist Maxwell used the power of social media to not only contact Lucas Holliday, but to invite Holliday to join him on stage at his upcoming concert in metro Detroit. Since then, Lucas has appeared on Good Morning America, NBC's *The Voice*, and a host of other national media outlets!

Some might call Lucas Holliday's story the perfect example of an overnight success. I would disagree. To me, Lucas Holliday is a testament of the power of doing it in the dark.

What does 'Doing it in the dark' mean?

Often successes that seem overnight, all of a sudden, or serendipitous are actually the work of practice and cultivation during seasons of obscurity. Many of us are in a space of doing it in the dark. Like Lucas, we are maintaining 'bread and butter' careers that keep the bills paid while we hustle and grind to birth the true dreams of our hearts. The habits, practices, and routines in the obscure spaces of our lives often set us up to occupy the dream spaces of our hearts. Here are some principles I've learned about doing it in the dark:

Principal #1: Do it because YOU love it, not in response to who approves of it.

Best-selling author Seth Godin was once asked why he blogged daily. He responded that blogging made him come alive. He went on to say that he was committed to blogging daily whether people read his writing or not. Doing it in the dark demands motivation rooted within. Being internally motivated will fuel your passion to pursue your craft and perfect your gift whether the world takes notice or not.

Principal #2: Discipline, Consistency, and Investment Required

In the dark is where you cultivate the habits and practices needed to sustain a presence in the light. Doing it in the dark requires ongoing learning and relentless dedication, time, energy, and investment toward perfecting your craft.

Principal #3: Remember: Darkness is temporary and light is coming.

Don't define yourself by where you are at the moment. Before he was an award-winning artist, Maxwell himself worked as a busboy clearing plates from tables. Until your desired change or dream takes flight, you may have to work jobs that meet your 'in the meantime' financial obligations. Don't be discouraged. Don't lose heart. Don't doubt your gifts, purpose, voice, or presence. Many visionaries experience obscurity before notoriety seasons.

Principal #4: Start where you are with what you know and what you have

Doing it in the dark means celebrating every opportunity, baby step, and growth moment. When I first started traveling and speaking, my first honorarium was a $10 Walgreens gift card. I drove away from that event feeling dismayed. I had prepared and delivered with excellence only to be given enough to buy a few rolls of bathroom tissue. At some point during my drive home, I remember my attitude changing. I stopped my pity party, and drove to Walgreens. I picked up some things for the house and said a prayer of thanks for the opportunity and gift I had been given. What you may be sowing in the dark as in-kind now, may form the basis of your next financial increase!

Tough Skin, Soft Heart Truth

Tough Skin: My dreams are worth my investment. I will celebrate every opportunity, growth step, and win on my journey.

Soft Heart: Doing it in the dark may bring with it days when I feel despair or dismay. In those moments, I will draw strength and renewal from watching, reading, and listening to the obscurity-to-notoriety journey of others.

SHANNON
COHEN
TOUGH SKIN, *Soft Heart*

If your organization is looking for a leadership spark, *look no further.*

Shannon Cohen speaks honestly and directly to leaders who are capable of excelling in every aspect of their life and work, but need a powerful reminder. Her message penetrates the invisible insecurities leaders bury beneath a skin that's been toughened by the rigors of expectations, responsibilities, and harsh realities. Whether she's consulting a team or speaking to an organization, Shannon communicates real strategies that bring out people's best selves.

As a strategist, innovator, and inspirational speaker, Shannon merges scholarship, practicality, and emotional intelligence, positioning leaders and organizations to thrive at the intersection of joy and purpose.

"SPEAK LIFE TO THE DREAMS OF YOUR OWN SOUL."
—SHANNON COHEN

Learn more and inquire about
hiring Shannon for your next event at

shannoncohen.com

KEEP THE **INSPIRATION**
ALIVE WITH MORE FROM

Shannon Cohen